C000174209

AYLESBURY REMEMBERED

KARL VAUGHAN

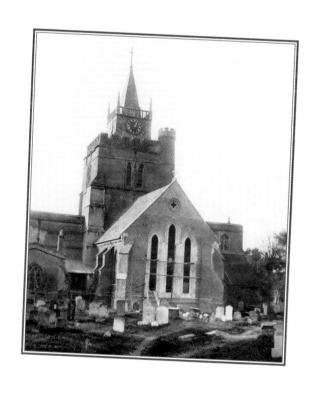

SUTTON PUBLISHING

Sutton Publishing Limited
Phoenix Mill · Thrupp · Stroud
Gloucestershire · GL5 2BU

First published 2005

Title page: St Mary's Church, *c.* 1860.
This photograph was taken during the
restoration of the church which was
undertaken by the architect Sir George
Gilbert Scott. St Mary's was in a bad and, in
places, dangerous state of repair. The works
carried out took over twenty years to
complete. *(Bucks County Museum)*

British Library Cataloguing in Publication Data
A catalogue record for this book is available from the
British Library.

ISBN 0-7509-3923-0

Typeset in 10.5/13.5 Photina.
Typesetting and origination by
Sutton Publishing Limited.
Printed and bound in England by
J.H. Haynes & Co. Ltd, Sparkford.

The fire brigade of printers Hazell, Watson & Viney, *c.* 1900. *(R.J. Johnson)*

CONTENTS

The original Tudor Market House, which was demolished in about 1808. *(K. Vaughan)*

JAMES PICKBURN,
PRINTER, BOOKSELLER, STATIONER,

ETC., ETC.,

TEMPLE STREET, AYLESBURY.

SCHOOL, COPY, CIPHERING, AND ACCOUNT BOOKS.

PERIODICALS REGULARLY SUPPLIED.

NEW BOOKS, MUSIC, ETC., PROCURED WEEKLY.

PRINTING OF EVERY DESCRIPTION,

(Letter-Press, Copper-Plate, and Lithographic) including Circulars, Cards, Catalogues, Posting Bills, Invoice Heads, &c., executed with neatness and despatch.

BOOKBINDING NEATLY EXECUTED.

☞ *Depository for the Society for Promoting Christian Knowledge.*

THE BUCKS HERALD
And UXBRIDGE ADVERTISER;

OR,

AGRICULTURAL JOURNAL & ADVERTISING CHRONICLE,

Circulating through Bucks, Beds, Berks, Oxon, Northants, and West Middlesex : with which is incorporated

THE WINDSOR AND ETON JOURNAL,

And contains latest intelligence at Home and abroad—Friday's London Markets—Original Letters from Paris—Ecclesiastical Intelligence—Latest Local News—Select Articles from the London Papers.—A SECOND EDITION is published in all cases of importance.

The Paper is Published every FRIDAY Evening, Price 4½d., or £1 per Annum.

All Advertisements and Communications addressed to the Publisher, J. PICKBURN, Aylesbury

AYLESBURY (near the County Hall).

——o——

JOSEPH PETTIT,

WHOLESALE AND RETAIL

Tea Dealer, Grocer, and Cheesemonger.

Wiltshire Bacon, Tongues, Fine York Hams, &c.   *Importer of Foreign Fruits.*

———

Families and Shops supplied on the most reasonable terms.

☞ *Purchasers for CASH may find all the advantages offered by London Houses without the trouble and expense of a journey to Town.*

Some adverts from a page in an 1853 street directory. (K. Vaughan)

INTRODUCTION

In this book I shall be covering the 100 years between the 1830s and the 1930s. It is a fascinating period of Aylesbury's history as it shows how the town grew to accommodate an increasing population. Not only is the period remarkable for what happened during the time but also we will see some amazing photographs, many of which are very high quality and give a real insight into how the town used to look. I have used many photographs from my own expanding collection, together with some from private collections and some from the Buckinghamshire County Museum's archive, along with some from the Bucks Local Studies collection. Most of my information is gathered from previous books on Aylesbury, in particular, Robert Gibbs' *History of Aylesbury* which was first printed in 1885. It contains many interesting and useful facts about the town. I have also spent six months reading through every *Bucks Herald* or *Bucks Advertiser & Aylesbury News* between the years 1837 and 1910 to find out what Aylesbury was like in those old times. It has proved a very interesting exercise and I have included some details of what I have discovered in various captions throughout the book.

In 1839 the Aylesbury to Cheddington railway was established, the station being in Railway Street. This provided the town with links to London and the north which brought not only convenience to the masses but also a booming trade with the markets of the capital. The journey to London for instance was significantly quicker and meant that produce would be fresher when it got to the markets. As is well known, the town is noted for producing the 'Aylesbury Duck'. This was a popular dish in the best London restaurants of the day. Not only was the coming of the railway important, but the construction of the New Road in 1826 (renamed to High Street in 1892) was a great improvement to Aylesbury. The buildings that were originally erected in the New Road were residential, but gradually, over the years, businesses started to crop up and buildings were either altered, or demolished and replaced with larger and more convenient premises. This happened for example with Longley's the drapers who were formerly in the Market Square. They moved into what was known as Tring Villas which stood on the corner of Britannia Street, facing New Road. In 1894 a whole new shopfront for this firm was erected by builders, Webster and Cannon.

During the 1840s the Old Gaol was demolished at the rear of the County Hall. This was done brick by brick and everything was sold off. At the time of the auction there were 1 million bricks for sale, together with every fixture and fitting associated with the old building. In similar fashion, the old Union Workhouse, which was on Oxford Road where Mount Street now stands, was demolished and sold off in many lots. New buildings for both the gaol and the Union Workhouse were built in Bierton Road. Throughout the Victorian period building materials were often recycled, as many of the fittings were made to a high standard and could easily be used again in the erection of new buildings.

The most profound change to Aylesbury's appearance came in 1864 when the Market Square lost all of the buildings that occupied the centre of the square. This was because of the formation of the Aylesbury Market Company in 1863. It was decided that the town would benefit from having purpose-built premises where trading could take place in a better, more modern environment. The White Hart Hotel at the bottom of the square was sold to the company by the owner, John Kersley Fowler, who incidentally was a member of the Market Company. As soon as the building was demolished work began on the Corn Exchange and the covered market to the rear. In the following year, 1865, the buildings in the centre of the square were swept away to leave an empty space. This also meant that the town no longer had a clock in the square. One of the buildings that was demolished was the Market House. It was an octagonal structure that was built in about 1809. On top of the building was a cupola, inside which was the bell. Just below it, on two sides, was the town clock. This was given to the town by Acton Tindal in 1851 when he became Lord of the Manor of Aylesbury with Bierton. For years after the Market House's demolition, people continued to miss the clock and every few weeks in the *Bucks Advertiser & Aylesbury News* letters were printed from people complaining and requesting that something be done about it. At the time of the construction of the Corn Exchange in 1864, plans were drawn up for a clock tower but when work was completed on the new Corn Exchange, no money was left to build it. Finally in 1876 work began on the present Clock Tower in the Market Square, the money being raised by public subscription. Everyone in the town was invited to put money towards the project, however modest the amount. Once completed in the following year, it was a striking addition to the town and today is one of Aylesbury's best-known landmarks.

Another major undertaking was the restoration of St Mary's Church between 1848 and the 1860s by the noted architect, Sir George Gilbert Scott. The state of the church at the commencement of the works was rather dangerous. The tower was most unsafe as it was supported by piers that were not perpendicular, largely because they were built with inadequate foundations. Each pier had to be shored up and carefully dismantled. The foundation pits were cut to a depth of 7ft and each base stone was surrounded by concrete, giving a good solid support. The same work was carried out on the piers on the north side of the Nave. Once the building was made safe, work began on the rest of the ancient structure. In 1852 a new wall surmounted by iron railings was built to mark the boundary of the churchyard. The work was carried out by Messrs Tyler and Co. from Dudley at a cost of £151. In 1858 the new cemetery was opened in Tring Road. Burials were still carried out in the old churchyard but only very occasionally.

A view of Market Square, *c.* 1915. *(K. Vaughan)*

During the Victorian period Aylesbury's trades were mainly lace making, basket making and, of course, duck breeding. In addition, all the usual trades associated with a market town were to be found: drapers, milliners, ironmongers, bootmakers and so on. In 1870 the town had its first major factory established – the English Condensed Milk Factory. It later became the Anglo-Swiss Condensed Milk Factory and then Nestlé. Three years before, in 1867, the printing firm of Watson & Hazell (later Hazell, Watson & Viney) established their works in an old silk mill in the California area of the town. Later on they moved into bigger and more modern premises near the Milk Factory on Tring Road.

To cater for all these working people, Aylesbury boasted more than eighty pubs, beerhouses and inns. Many of the pubs and beerhouses were run by the owners to provide them with an additional income. For instance in the 1850s Jesse Ward who was a builder also ran the King's Head Inn. By the end of the nineteenth century the licensing authorities clamped down on the number of licensed premises in the town because of the increasing problem of drunkenness. The number of pubs soon started to reduce to between sixty and seventy.

With the addition of factories to the town, an inevitable increase in the population took place. A building boom which started in the 1870s saw the emergence of estates like Victoria Park, Manor Park, Queen's Park and in the 1920s, Southcourt. Many houses were also built along all the principal routes into Aylesbury. Something of historical interest was found in 1890 when a house was being built on Rickfords

An early nineteenth-century view of the old Bucks Infirmary at the top of the Buckingham and Bicester roads. *(Bucks County Museum)*

Hill on land belonging to jeweller and silversmith Thomas Field. During the digging of the foundations large pieces of masonry were found, together with some stone steps. These were the remains of the old Franciscan Friarage which stood in that area. Its exact location is not known but it was certainly in the vicinity of Friarage Passage, hence the name. Remains were also found during the digging work carried out for the installation of sewers in Bourbon Street. It is a shame that Friars Square Shopping Centre completely obliterated much of that area during its construction in the 1960s – who knows what would have been found if a proper archaeological survey had been carried out?

I hope this book proves to be as interesting to you as it has been for me to compile. It shows very clearly how much Aylesbury has changed over the years. It was such a small place!

Karl Vaughan, 2005

1

The Early Years
1830–99

The Market Square, 1865. *(R.J. Johnson)*

PROGRAMME
OF THE
CORONATION
FESTIVAL.

All Persons intending to Dine are to assemble in Kingsbury, at Three o'Clock precisely, and then to walk in procession to the Dining Tables, (except the Infirm, who are to take their places at their respective Tables). All Persons must wear their Tickets, and bring their own Knives and Forks.

The following Toasts will be announced by a Flourish of Trumpets :---

THE QUEEN,
The Queen Dowager and the rest of the Royal Family.
The Lord of the Manor.

At half-past Five o'Clock the Amusements will commence, in the following Order :

FIRST.
A DONKEY RACE FOR A BRIDLE,
The Second in to have a Pair of Spurs.
SECOND.
Jumping in Sacks,
FOR A SMOCK-FROCK.
THIRD.
RACE FOR WOMEN UNDER 30 YEARS OF AGE, FOR GOWN PIECES.
FOURTH.
BOYS TO EAT ROLLS AND TREACLE, FOR A SMOCK-FROCK.
FIFTH.
JINGLING MATCH, FOR A WAISTCOAT.
SIXTH.
A Foot Race for Men above Fifty,
FOR TOBACCO: THREE PRIZES.
SEVENTH.
A FOOT RACE FOR WOMEN, BETWEEN 30 & 50,
FOR ONE POUND OF BEST TEA.
EIGHTH.
WHEELBARROW RACE FOR A NEW HAT,
The Competitors to be Blindfolded.
NINTH.
A RACE FOR MEN BETWEEN FIFTY AND SIXTY, FOR A SMOCK-FROCK
TENTH.
Ditto for WOMEN above Fifty, for half a pound of Snuff.
ELEVENTH.
A Donkey Race for a Bridle,
The last placed to take the Prize : No Man to ride his own Steed.
Boys dipping for Oranges.   *Climbing Poles for Legs of Mutton, &c.*
To Conclude with a Brilliant DISPLAY of FIRE-WORKS.

N.B. It is particularly requested that no Fire-Works be let off until after the Public Exhibition, that Females may not be annoyed.

Persons wishing to contend for any of the above Prizes, may send in their Names to the Committee at the White Hart Inn.

By Order of the Committee.
"GOD SAVE THE QUEEN!"

GIBBS, PRINTER, AYLESBURY.

A poster advertising the festivities to mark the Coronation of Queen Victoria in 1837.
(Bucks County Museum)

An engraving of St Mary's Church in 1843 by N. Whittock. This was drawn before work began on the church's restoration. It shows the large east window before it was removed and placed in the grounds of Green End House. *(R.J. Johnson)*

Aylesbury railway station, April 1856. The Aylesbury to Cheddington line opened on 10 June 1839. The weather was fine that day and people took journeys to and from Cheddington all day. The station building stood at the end of Railway Street until it was demolished in 1889 when the new station opened in the High Street. Now there are virtually no remains of the site as it was closed in 1953 and eventually everything was removed. *(Bucks County Museum)*

Market Square, *c.* 1860. This unique scene was photographed from the first floor of the old White Hart Hotel and shows the square with the buildings that occupied the centre. The Market House can be seen at the far end of the block. This was built in about 1809 and replaced an earlier, timber-framed structure (a drawing of this is shown on page 3). The clock above the Market House was given to the town in 1851 by Acton Tindal when he became Lord of the Manor. At the time this view was taken, a Market Company was being formed by the main businessmen of the town. It was widely felt that the Market Square had become too inconvenient and a decision was made to find a better and more modern place for trade. The company bought the site of the White Hart which was sold to it by the owner, John Kersley Fowler, who was also on the committee. The building was dismantled in the spring of 1864 and everything sold off – even the turf from the lawns at the rear! The profits made were put towards the building of the new Corn Exchange with a covered market at the rear. In February 1866 work began on the demolition of the old Market House. Firstly the clock was carefully removed and put into storage

where it remained for some years. The building materials were auctioned off and reached a final price of £108. The next buildings to go were the shops of Mr Kingham and Mr Longley (shown on page 14) in October 1866. The *Bucks Herald* offices and the Oxford Arms pub (next to the Green Man) were demolished and a large new building was constructed on the site. This would become Mr Kingham's new premises. Last to go was a picturesque building known as the 'Cage' which ironically had recently been repaired. This building was used in previous years as a lock-up for people committing trivial offences. In late November 1866 the building was demolished using heavyweight balls. At first a 40-pounder was tried to no effect. Then a 50-pounder, still nothing. A 60-pounder was tried and still the building stood firm. Finally a 70-pounder was brought in and the building gave way. This old structure seemed to have been built well. With the last building gone it left the square completely empty and it was not long before people began to miss their fine town clock. (*Bucks County Museum*)

Above: This is a view of the buildings that occupied the centre of the Market Square, *c.* 1860. Waterloo House, as this building was called, stood roughly where the Clock Tower is today. An interesting fact about these buildings is that they had cellars. One may notice when walking down Market Square how uneven the surface is under foot. This is probably due to constant rebuilding over the centuries. Mr Longley's draper's shop, seen on the left, eventually moved into larger premises in the High Street. (*Bucks County Museum*)

New Road (High Street), *c.* 1860. This view gives a good example of how residential the road was in those days. The large house on the left was occupied by John Griffits, then the High Bailiff of the County Court. Every building seen here has now gone. Where the walled garden is, the post office now stands. The only building recognisable in this view is St Mary's Church which looms on the horizon. (*Bucks County Museum*)

New Road (High Street), *c.* 1860. This view appears rather desolate as the road was yet to be built on further down the hill. To the left is the entrance to Railway Street which at the time led to the Aylesbury to Cheddington station. Just beyond the horse and cart is the Chandos Inn. It stood on the corner of Exchange Street, a road which was barely in existence as it was then just a narrow lane leading to the rear of the White Hart in Market Square. It would be a few years yet before anything more was built further down the road. *(Bucks County Museum)*

The White Hart Hotel in Market Square, *c.* 1860. This was a very old inn which dated from the Tudor period. Originally the façade consisted of three gables with each floor overhanging the lower one. To the rear were extensive grounds stretching right down to Bear Brook. The building was modernised in 1814 with stone taken from Eythrope House which was being demolished at the time. The portico was from the stables of that house. The former Corn Exchange, now the Town Hall, stands on the site. *(K. Vaughan)*

The Market House, c. 1864. This building only stood here for about 60 years. The previous building on the site (shown on page 3) was timber framed and dated from the sixteenth century. It is said that the bell from that Market House came from the Grey Friars Monastery, which was demolished during the Civil War. It was then transferred to the new Market House and installed into the Clock Tower. If the bell still remains there today, then we are hearing the same sound that the friars heard 500 years ago. (*Bucks County Museum*)

The newly built Corn Exchange in 1865. The foundation stone was laid on 13 July 1864 by Lord Carrington and the building opened on 11 October 1865. It was designed by architect David Brandon and consisted of a covered market with a corn exchange which was through the arches at the rear, and the Town Hall which was immediately to the left of the main entrance. *(Bucks County Museum)*

Below: Aylesbury from the fields that would later become Southcourt, *c.* 1870. Just below the centre, the line of the Great Western Railway can be seen with a row of trees overlooking California Brook in front of it. St Mary's Church stands proud on the horizon, dwarfing everything around it. The large building on the far left is the old Silk Mill which was built on the site of the old Union Workhouse. Just below the big tree are cottages in Green End, long since gone. *(R.J. Johnson)*

Hale Leys Chapel in New Road (High Street), *c.* 1870. The chapel was opened in 1707 long before New Road was laid down. It faced pleasant meadows (called the Hale Leys) with just a track leading to it. Over the years the chapel needed constant repair and in the 1870s a decision was made to demolish this old building and construct the Congregational church on the same site. It opened on 19 March 1874. A view of this church can be seen on page 26. (*Bucks County Museum*)

An empty Market Square, *c.* 1870. When the square lost its fine clock people began to complain in the newspapers of the day. Eventually it was decided to raise money by public subscription to build a Clock Tower. The plans were actually drawn up and were ready at the time of the Corn Exchange's construction but with all the purchasing of the buildings in the centre of the square, no money was left over at the end of the scheme. When enough money was raised during 1876, work began on the Clock Tower. (*Bucks County Museum*)

Kingsbury, c. 1870. These are the premises of Joseph Goss who, apart from being a plumber, was a man of many talents. He did signwriting, paper hanging, glazing and painting. The lane to the left of the building is George Street and just visible on the far left is the Red Lion (now the Hobgoblin). Just out of view on the far right was the Basketmakers Arms – a pub which was demolished in the 1880s to make way for the Victoria Club. *(Bucks County Museum)*

The English Condensed Milk Factory, 1870. This is an early view and shows the original factory buildings. Construction started on the factory at the end of New Road (High Street) in May 1870 and was carried out by Mr Haddon of Walton Street. The factory opened in September the same year. Condensed milk was quite a novelty at the time as it lasted for weeks, whereas fresh milk perished in just a few days. Both of these buildings were demolished in 1899 when the factory was rebuilt. *(M. Sale)*

St Mary's Church, *c. 1870*. Here we see the church during its restoration. At the start of the works the building was in a dangerous state of repair. The tower was unsafe because the supporting pillars were apparently built on hardly any foundations at all. This problem was one of the first to be sorted out. Later on, more architectural work was carried out. The large window seen here was inserted, replacing a more elaborate one. The old window now stands in the grounds of Green End House on Rickfords Hill. *(Bucks County Museum)*

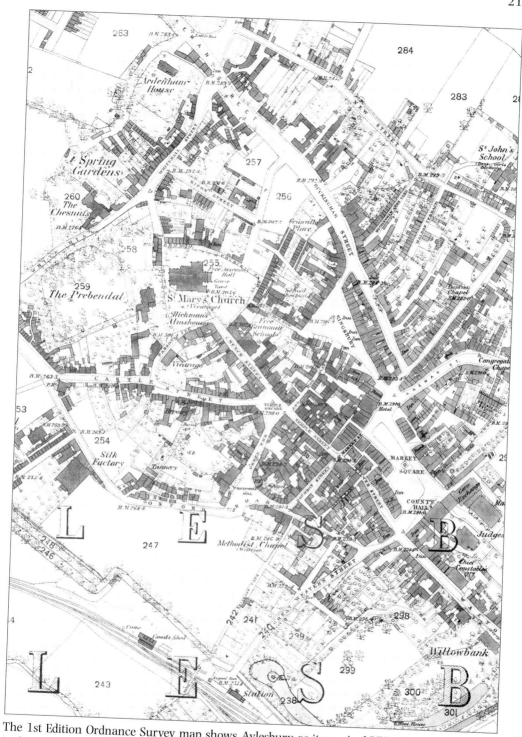

The 1st Edition Ordnance Survey map shows Aylesbury as it was in 1878. Shown in this view is the station of the Great Western Railway which opened in 1862. The Silk Factory (bottom left centre), Mount Street and St Mary's School were built on the site of the old Union Workhouse. The new workhouse opened in 1844 on Bierton Road and still exists today; it is now known as the Tindal Centre. A view of the Silk Factory can be seen on page 17.
(Reproduced from the 1878 Ordnance Survey Map)

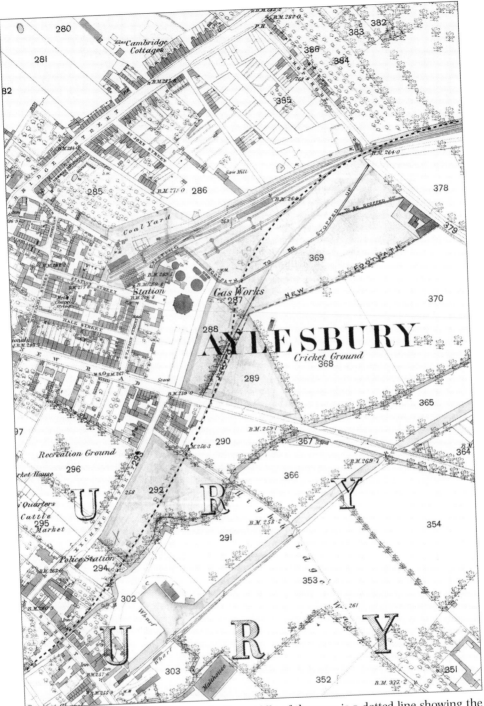

Another view of the town in 1878. In the middle of the map is a dotted line showing the proposed railway line which would join the two town stations. The line starts at the crossing in Park Street and then curves downwards to where the new High Street station would be built, and continues across the road following the line of Exchange Street, across Walton Street and eventually joining on to the GWR station. This plan was never undertaken, although rails were actually laid along Exchange Street in preparation for the link but were later buried. *(Reproduced from the 1878 Ordnance Survey Map)*

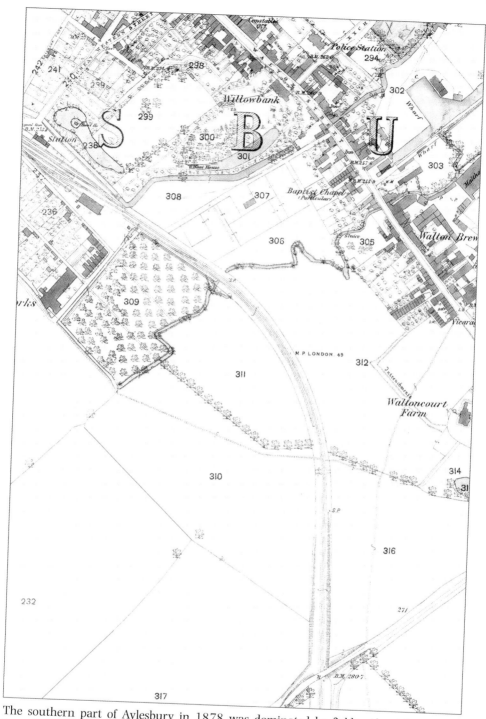

The southern part of Aylesbury in 1878 was dominated by fields. About forty years later the Southcourt housing estate would be built to the left of the railway line. Walton Street is visible to the north of Waltoncourt Farm. Houses occupied both sides of the road in those days. Two of the larger sites on that street were Walton Brewery, seen just below the canal basin, and Willowbank, an old house with extensive gardens and two small lakes. It must have been a beautiful place to walk round. *(Reproduced from the 1878 Ordnance Survey Map)*

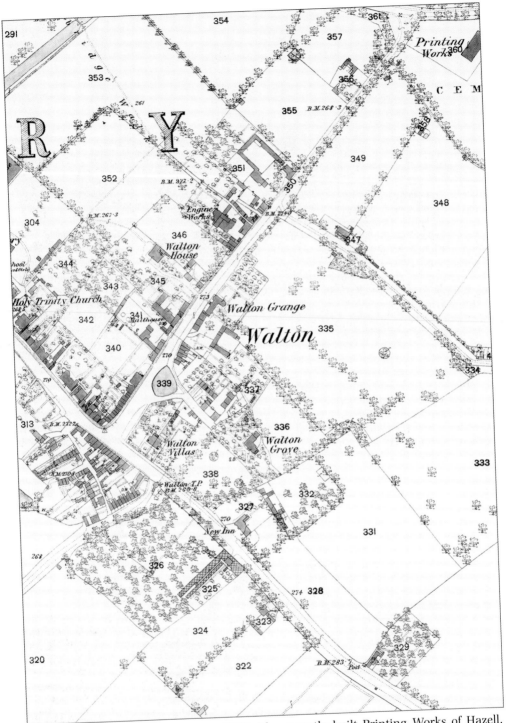

We now take a look at Walton in 1878. The recently built Printing Works of Hazell, Watson & Viney are seen at the top of the map with Walton Road stretching downwards to join Walton Street and Wendover Road. All on its own at the bottom, fronting Wendover Road, is the Three Pigeons public house which is no longer there. In the next decade it would be accompanied by several new houses built for the extending town of Aylesbury. The building goes on. . . . (*Reproduced from the 1878 Ordnance Survey Map*)

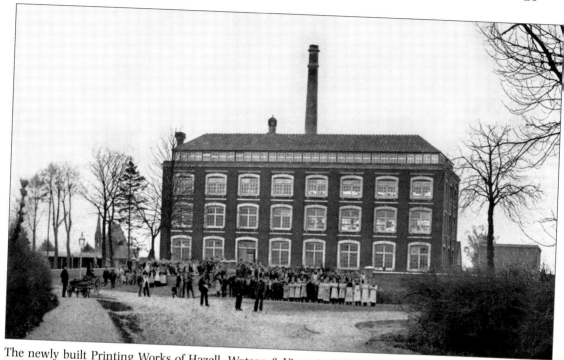

The newly built Printing Works of Hazell, Watson & Viney in 1878. The firm moved from its old site on California to this new one on Tring Road. This view was taken from New Road (High Street) with Tring Road off to the left and Walton Road on the right. This was the first building to be put up on the site and over the next few years would be altered and added to considerably. The firm was the major employer in Aylesbury for many years and the site covered a huge area. Everything has since been demolished and the only reminder of what was once there is the mosaic company name on a wall in Victoria Street and the old factory entrance pillars which now form the entrance to Tesco. (*Bucks County Museum*)

Market Square, 1880. It took ten years before the Clock Tower was finally put up in the square. During the summer of 1876 a house-to-house collection was made to raise the required funds for construction (the final amount raised during subscription was £882 10s 11d). Tenders were sent in by three local builders for the works. Messrs Cooper (builder) and Cowles (stonemason) won with their tender of £586 10s. Work began in June 1876 and the building work was completed in December of that year. Because of the wet weather at that time of year, work was delayed as the tower was too damp for the clock to be safely fitted. In June 1877 it was finally installed by clockmakers Field & Sons, who refurbished the clock, giving it two extra faces so that now the time could be seen on all four sides of the tower. (*K. Vaughan*)

New Road (High Street), *c.* 1880. The Congregational church was built between 1873 and 1874 on the site of Hale Leys chapel. The builders were Messrs Cooper and Ball. A view of this old building is seen on page 18. (*K. Vaughan*)

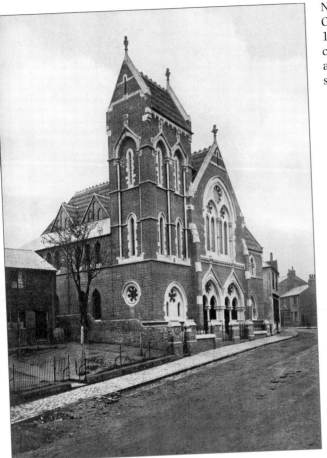

Below: California seen from the fields that would later be occupied by the Southcourt housing estate, *c.* 1880. The large building with the chimney was originally a silk mill and was adapted for use as the original printing works of Hazell, Watson & Viney who established their business in Aylesbury in 1867. When the new factory was built in Tring Road in 1878 the old factory was used as its ink works. On the far right is Walton Vicarage (now Walton House) with Holy Trinity Church just to the left of it. It is difficult to see the church, as at the time the tower was not yet built. It was completed in 1887. A view of Holy Trinity Church can be seen on page 31. (*Bucks County Museum*)

This page from an 1886 calendar gives a fine example of the skills of Victorian engravers. *(R.J. Johnson)*

Buckingham Street, *c.* 1885. This end of the street was originally called Back Street because many of the premises in Kingsbury had their rear entrances here. In this view there are five pubs; on the left are the Two Brewers (in the foreground), the Rose & Crown (behind the trees) and the Harrow at the far end; on the right are the Eagle and the Cock, both of which had their main entrances in Kingsbury. There were many businesses down here too, such as a whitesmith (someone who works in white metals such as tin), upholsterer, bookbinder, chemist, coal merchant, coach builder . . . the list goes on. *(M. Sale)*

A view along the canal taken from the bridge at New Road (High Street) looking towards the canal basin in the late 1880s. The bridge seen here connected Highbridge Walk with a footpath that ran across the fields where Queen's Park was later built, and came out next to the Old Millwrights Arms in Walton Road. *(Bucks County Museum)*

The Ark pub on the corner of Station Street, *c. 1888.* Taken from Britannia Street this view shows the pub being covered by bill posters Joseph Taylor and his grandson Francis Slade. Both of these men were town criers in Aylesbury. Francis took over the role when his grandfather died. Francis is seen in his outfit on page 48. *(M. Sale)*

The London & North Western Railway station on Railway Street, 1888. This photograph was taken shortly before this building was demolished. When the new station opened in the High Street the following year, this old site was used for cattle pens. *(M. Sale)*

On 9 July 1889 the Shah of Persia and Prince Albert Victor (later Duke of Clarence) visited Aylesbury. They drove through the town on their way from Halton to Waddesdon. It seems people needed little encouragement to decorate their town in those days. Along the whole route various banners and flags were displayed from the buildings. Here we see the Market Square decorated for the event. Also of note is the balcony on the building to the left. A possible reason for its existence was to allow people to get a good view of the hangings that used to take place outside the County Hall. By 1889, though, hangings had long since ceased in the Market Square. (Bucks County Museum)

The Victoria Club, c. 1890. The first committee, nominated by Baron Rothschild, met at Walton Grange in February 1887. The baron wanted to provide a working men's club for the town at his own expense. It was built on the site of the old Basketmakers Arms pub in Kingsbury. (Bucks County Museum)

Holy Trinity Church, Walton Street, *c.* 1890. The church was built in 1845 by local builder, Jesse Ward. This photograph was taken shortly after the tower was added to the front in 1887. *(R.J. Johnson)*

Below: Cutting the first turf of the Metropolitan Railway extension by Stoke Road on 5 May 1890. During the works, temporary rails were laid between Aylesbury and Great Missenden to serve the navvies. A steam digger, or as it was commonly called, the 'railway devil', was used for the excavation work. It was capable of shifting 300 wagon loads of ballast per day which made for speedy progress. The new line was opened on 1 September 1892. *(Bucks County Museum)*

A crowded Market Square as Queen Victoria passes through Aylesbury on her way to Waddesdon Manor on 14 May 1890. Her Majesty arrived at Aylesbury station at 1.10 p.m. and as she stepped from the train Baron Ferdinand de Rothschild greeted her and remarked on the fineness of the weather. The Queen responded by saying, 'Yes, I always take fine weather with me'. (R.J. Johnson)

Every part of the town was decorated for the occasion of Queen Victoria's visit. Here we see Bicester Road during the festivities. Also at certain locations, arches were erected for the Queen to pass under. The town must have looked quite amazing. (Centre for Bucks Studies)

Women hard at work in the bookbinding department of printers Hazell, Watson & Viney, *c.* 1890. The firm was established in London in 1839 by William Paul and was bought by George Watson in 1843. Walter Hazell entered the business in 1863 and in 1867 George Watson jnr came to Aylesbury to establish a new branch of the business. The premises in California had only three employees to start with but was soon to become the biggest employer in the town. *(R.J. Johnson)*

The canal basin, *c.* 1890. The canal was completed in 1814 and was a great asset to the town. It meant that people could transport heavy items to different parts of the country far more easily than ever before. When the railway came to Aylesbury in 1839 it was a great rival to the canal. Nowadays of course the canal is used mainly for leisure activities and is quite popular with cyclists, joggers, anglers and walkers. *(Centre for Bucks Studies)*

Looking towards Oxford Road (now Friarage Road) from Mill Way, *c.* 1890. The building on the right is St Mary's School, which has recently relocated to the new Fairford Leys estate. Just to the left of it is a pub that stood at the bottom of Castle Street, the Rising Sun, which was an old rambling building. Also visible are the cottages that faced Oxford Road for hundreds of years until the 1960s when they were swept away for road widening. *(Bucks County Museum)*

The Chestnuts, *c.* 1895. This large house stood halfway up White Hill and had extensive grounds. Later on its name was changed to The Gate House and the building remained there until the late 1940s when it was demolished. Much of the site has since been built on and the name has been preserved in Gatehouse Road, which joins Bicester Road with Friarage Road. *(Centre for Bucks Studies)*

Buckingham Arms yard, 1897. The pub, which is on the left, could well have got its name from the Duke of Buckingham who was Lord of the Manor in the early nineteenth century. On the 1809 map of Aylesbury the pub is shown under a different name, the Black Boy. This yard leads from Buckingham Street (which is through the gap) through to Cambridge Place. The pub remains there to this day although it now known as the Emperor's Lounge. (Bucks County Museum)

view along the platform of Aylesbury High Street station, c. 1897. The station moved from its old site Railway Street in 1889. At the end of the platform is the way out to the station forecourt where arriages would wait to pick up travellers. Note the advertisement boards on the walls. (Leicestershire ounty Council)

Here we see the Railway Tavern in Great Western Street in 1898 before it was completely rebuilt later that year. It was then a rather small and plain building that had been designed by Guest Luckett – the same man who designed the Masonic Hall in Ripon Street. (*Bucks County Museum*)

This is how the Railway Tavern looked after being rebuilt. The new building was larger than it predecessor and was able to cater for more people. Another change was the name which was altered t the Railway Hotel. Sadly this elaborate example of Victorian architecture is no longer with us as it wa demolished in 1966 to make way for the Friars Square Shopping Centre. (*Bucks County Museum*)

2

A New Century
1900–9

A church parade of the Aylesbury Territorials in Market Square, 25 July 1909.
(K. Vaughan)

On 8 January 1900 members of the Royal Bucks Hussars (commanded by Lord Chesham) assembled in Market Square to prepare for departure to South Africa to serve in the Boer War. They had a great send-off, and a box of cigars was given to the men to share between them. There were great cheers from the assembled crowd at the railway station in Great Western Street as the train left the platform. One wonders how many of these men returned after their service. (K. Vaughan)

The approach to Aylesbury from the Hartwell Road, c. 1900. This view is from the bridge which today is next to Churchill Avenue. It shows very well how much smaller the town was in those days (K. Vaughan)

Looking towards White Hill, 1900. These cottages stood in a part of town that was popular with breeders of the famous Aylesbury Duck. A well-known breeder of the time was 'Ducky' Weston who lived in one of the cottages on the left. The middle cottage with the false central window was once the Seven Stars pub which was closed by the time this photograph was taken. *(K. Vaughan)*

On 30 January 1901 the proclamation of King Edward VII was read from the steps of County Hall in Market Square by the High Sheriff of Buckinghamshire, Sir Robert Grenville Harvey, in front of hundreds of people who had gathered for the event. *(Bucks County Museum)*

Looking down Walton Street from the town, *c.* 1900. This picturesque view shows how narrow the street was and that it was fronted by some very old buildings. The white house on the right with the bay windows was a Regency house called Walton Cottage. The entrance to Exchange Street is opposite the tall tree in the centre. *(K. Vaughan)*

Further down Walton Street, *c.* 1900. Just behind the tower of Holy Trinity Church is the vicarage, built in 1862. The architect was David Brandon. He seems to have been a busy man in the 1860s as he designed the Town Hall and Corn Exchange, the Clock Tower in Market Square and the Royal Bucks Hospital. The house nearest the camera was demolished in 1927 to make way for Walton Parish Hall. The rest of the buildings stretching up the road here still survive. *(R.J. Johnson)*

Walton Street looking towards town, *c.* 1900. The last building on the left had for years been used to advertise various businesses with the wall facing having bill posters pasted on; at times the whole wall was painted in big letters. Walton Terrace (stretching up on the right) has no railings along it. It is surprising that they were not put up sooner as there were many accidents along here with people, particularly drunks, falling into the road. This scene has changed a great deal as Holy Trinity Church and the house on the right now overlook a dual carriageway. *(R.J. Johnson)*

The Union Workhouse in Bierton Road, *c.* 1900. Aylesbury had a workhouse in Oxford Road (now Friarage Road) that was built in the 1820s but by the 1840s it had become inadequate and a decision was made to build a better one in a different location. Bierton Road was the favoured site and the new workhouse opened in 1844 and was in operation until 1947 when the Poor Law system ended by Act of Parliament. It has since become the Tindal Centre for psychiatric and psychological treatment. *(Bucks County Museum)*

Nestlé factory, *c.* 1900. Established by the English Condensed Milk Company, the factory opened in 1870. Five years later the name was changed to the Anglo-Swiss Condensed Milk Company. The buildings seen here were built in 1899 when the Nestlé company took over the running of the factory. Park Street can be seen on the left going over the canal bridge. On the far right is the High Street. *(M. Sale)*

Bierton Road, *c.* 1900. These houses or 'villa residences' as they were described at the time, were built during the 1880s and 1890s. The entrance to Manor Park can be seen just by the tree in the centre. Manor Park was begun in the 1880s and was laid out in plots where houses were built. The estate was largely complete by about 1920. Stretching up Bierton Road on the right is the wall of the Manor House. *(R.J. Johnson)*

The Great Tree on Wendover Road, *c.* 1900. This elm was a local landmark and was about 200 years old. A few yards up the road is a milestone which is now on the opposite side of the road near the turning for Elm Farm. The tree was felled in October 1946. *(Bucks County Museum)*

Aylesbury Fire Brigade's new steam fire engine is pictured here in the yard of the George Hotel in Market Square. It was bought by funds raised in the town in 1899 and proved a very useful piece of equipment. *(Bucks County Museum)*

Above: Bourbon Street, *c.* 1900. This view looks towards Market Square; the Round House at the end of the High Street can be seen through the gap. The large Georgian building on the right was a grocery store and wine merchant's run by M.T. Cocks from 1901. He took over the business from Mr Facer. Miles Thomas Cocks was from the same family that was a partner in Jones & Cocks ironmongers in Market Square. *(Bucks County Museum)*

The Baptist Chapel in Walton Street, *c.* 1900. The chapel was rebuilt in 1895 and stood opposite the canal basin. Just beyond the chapel to the right are cottages in what was Chapel Row. Everything has now disappeared to be replaced by the second carriageway of Walton Street. *(Bucks County Museum)*

The fire brigade of printers Hazell, Watson & Viney in Walton Road, *c.* 1900. This is viewed from the entrance to Turnfurlong and in the background stands the Old Millwrights Arms. Just to the left of the picture was another pub called the Millwrights Arms. It is unusual to have two pubs with virtually the same name next door to each other. Nowadays there is only one Millwrights Arms and it is a newer building than the one shown here. *(R.J. Johnson)*

High Street, *c.* 1900. The name of this road was changed from New Road in 1892. The change came about because the road was no longer new as it had been in existence since 1826. Here we see the street viewed from the very top end. On the left is one of Aylesbury's many long lost pubs, the Rothschilds Arms, which was not there for long. Opposite there is the Crown Hotel. *(K. Vaughan)*

Rickfords Hill, *c.* 1900. The man with the pony and trap is pig breeder Reuben Dorrell, who has just visited Thorp's the bacon factor. The large house on the left is Green End House. (*K. Vaughan*)

High Street, *c.* 1900. This is viewed from the very end of the road looking towards the Printing Works of Hazell, Watson & Viney which can just be seen through the trees. The wall stretching down on the left surrounded the Nestlé factory. On the other side of the road are tall trees, beyond which were fields that were later to be built on as part of Queen's Park together with more houses fronting High Street. (*K. Vaughan*)

This is an interesting view of the town from Queen's Park, *c.* 1900. The roads have only just been laid out on land that was known as Bentalls Hill. Highbridge Road is seen going down the hill to the left with Prince's Road branching off it. In the distance are the old gas works that were off Railway Street and on the horizon behind them is St John's Church which stood in Cambridge Street. A later view of Highbridge Road can be seen on page 90. *(Bucks County Museum)*

Temple Square during the coronation of Edward VII in August 1902. As with earlier royal events that had been celebrated in the town, Aylesbury was lavishly decorated with flags and banners. There was also a procession which was headed by the Printing Works Band. *(K. Vaughan)*

Mr Francis Slade, the town crier, in the Market Square during the coronation festivities for King Edward VII on 10 August 1902.

As well as being town crier, he was also a bill poster. His grandfather, Joseph Taylor, was town crier before him and this job was passed on to Francis on Taylor's death in the mid-1890s.
(K. Vaughan)

Buckingham Street, c. 1904. On the left is the large warehouse belonging to Gulliver's wine merchants. Their main premises were round in Kingsbury, in the same buildings as two former pubs, the Royal Oak and the Cock Inn. The pub opposite the warehouse is the Rose & Crown, which closed its doors in the 1930s when Chamberlin's carriage works next door expanded their business. (K. Vaughan)

The canal between High Street and Park Street, *c.* 1904. The old bridge seen here was not replaced until 1906. Many such bridges still exist down the canal to Marsworth and are testament to the quality of workmanship. Beyond the hedge on the right is the Nestlé factory. *(K. Vaughan)*

St Mary's Square, *c.* 1904. One could easily mistake this view for a recent one as these cottages have hardly changed in appearance in the last hundred years. The railings and churchyard wall were put up in 1852. One reason given for this was the fact that children from the nearby grammar school used to play frequently in the churchyard, damaging things. *(K. Vaughan)*

A busy Market Square, *c.* 1904. There is some activity at the top of the square with lots of men crowding round something – possibly a sheep sale. Livestock were often sold at this end of the square in those days. *(K. Vaughan)*

Flint Cottage in Granville Place, 1904. One of Aylesbury's more individual houses, it was built in 1854. Just above the front door is a stone with the initials JMW and the year inscribed into it. A known builder in the town around the 1850s was Jesse Ward who built Walton Church. It is likely he was responsible for the construction of this cottage. Also of note is the material used in the façade of the cottage, which is flint. This was also used extensively in the building of Walton Church. (K. Vaughan)

A peaceful Market Square in the early part of 1904. In July of that year Rowe & Co., the ironmonger's, changed its name to Jones & Cocks, a name which is familiar to locals as the firm is still trading in the town. (K. Vaughan)

Castle Street, c. 1904. This street was for many centuries the principal route into Aylesbury from Oxford. Because of this, many pubs and inns were established up and down the road to cater for tradesmen and visitors. The Black Horse was a popular inn that stood there for many years. It has long since closed. (K. Vaughan)

A quiet High Street, *c.* 1904. The High Street station opened in June 1889. The old station in Railway Street was subsequently demolished and the site was used as a cattle siding for many years. Now nothing whatsoever remains of the High Street station as it was removed together with the railway tracks in the 1960s. Now Vale Park Drive and Upper Hundreds Way go over the old site. *(K. Vaughan)*

A view of the edge of town taken from the Great Western Railway footbridge, *c.* 1904. All the houses in the distance are situated in Oxford Road and Green End. Nowadays this part of Oxford Road is known as Rickfords Hill. Just below the big tree on the left is the Wheatsheaf pub – the sign is just noticeable between the first-floor windows. This view illustrates how dense these parts of Aylesbury were, with many people crammed into quite small dwellings. *(K. Vaughan)*

A horse and trap belonging to the Aylesbury Steam Laundry on its way down the High Street, *c.* 1904. The building behind is the Nestlé factory with the manager's house in the foreground. These buildings were a fine example of late Victorian design. In about 1962 the central part of the factory was demolished and replaced by a large tower block. The factory has recently closed and in December 2004 the rest of the old buildings were scandalously demolished, leaving just the 1960s block standing. *(K. Vaughan)*

The canal from Highbridge Walk, *c.* 1904. The houses seen in the centre of frame are Coronation Villas, put up at about the time of King Edward VII's Coronation in 1902. In the field next to them, more houses would soon be built to complete the line fronting the canal. *(K. Vaughan)*

A fine sunny day in Market Square, *c.* 1904. The name of Sarsons is seen painted on the building in the distance. It was the name of an ironmonger's formerly known as Learner & Sarsons. The two large warehouses were built on the site of a Tudor inn called the Black Swan which was pulled down in 1883. The business was later taken over by M.H. Bradford. It moved to smaller premises in the High Street in 1935 when this end block was demolished to make way for Market House. (*K. Vaughan*)

A steam-driven roundabout in Kingsbury, *c.* 1904. This photograph was taken during the Michaelmas Fair which was held annually in Aylesbury and consisted of many different stalls being put up both in Kingsbury and Market Square. Entertainment was also laid on for the people of the town. (*K. Vaughan*)

Livestock for sale in Market Square, c. 1904. These cattle look rather relaxed standing there but the newspapers of the day suggest that the beasts were not always quite so well behaved. There were many instances of cattle bolting when being led through the square. One amusing story was of a cow which ended up going through Fields the jewellers in Market Square, managing to negotiate its way right through to the lane at the back! It must have been quite a shock for any customers in there at the time, not to mention the shopkeeper. (K. Vaughan)

During the morning of 23 December 1904, Aylesbury had its worst rail disaster. It was a foggy morning and a newspaper train from London came into the station at around 4.30 a.m. It was said to have been travelling at a speed of 60mph. When it came to the bend near the station, it left the rails and ploughed on to the neighbouring ones. A mail train coming from the opposite direction then collided with the wreckage. Four men were killed in the accident and an inquiry was held soon afterwards. (K. Vaughan)

This photograph was used during the inquest into the railway disaster to show the bends in the tracks that were a contributing factor to the tragedy. To prevent such an accident happening again, work was soon started on modifying the tracks. This view also shows a part of Aylesbury that has long since disappeared. In the centre are cottages in Prospect Place, which was off Walton Street. The piece of ground to the right was locally known as 'Humpy Bumpy Field' because of the many earthworks in the area. (K. Vaughan)

Above: Walton House, 1905. This building stood in fine grounds near the Millwrights pub in Walton Road. It was the home of Thomas Parrott and his large family. As well as being a solicitor in the town, he also had his own brewery. The name is still familiar today in Aylesbury in the law firm of Parrott & Coales. The house was demolished in 1947 when a technical college was built on the site. Today the area of Redwood Drive and Laurel Way occupies the site. *(K. Vaughan)*

An early Edwardian view of Temple Street. The large building on the left is the Literary Institute which was opened by Lord Rothschild on 22 October 1903. Facing the street at the end is the large premises of wine merchant M.T. Cocks. *(Bucks County Museum)*

Looking down the High Street, *c.* 1905. The large building on the left was the shop of Ethel Smith, milliner. She must have had a good trade, as most women wore hats at the time. This part of the street was still a mixture of businesses and private dwellings at the time. Note the large trees and front walls on the right. (*K. Vaughan*)

Tring Road from the end of High Street, *c.* 1905. These are the Printing Works of Hazell, Watson & Viney with the manager's house on the right. The single-storey Machinery Hall (next to the house) later had four more storeys added to it. The original 1878 building with the large chimney is seen in the centre. The block to the left was added in 1885. Across the road other large buildings were built in the coming years to cater for this ever expanding business. The firm produced millions of books during its lifetime and employed thousands of people. (*K. Vaughan*)

Stoke Road, *c.* 1905. In the distance the road is seen going over the railway bridge. In those days the road led on to farmland which would later become the Southcourt estate. Mr Harding seems to have afforded himself the services of a good signwriter for the front of his shop on the left. This scene is a far cry from today, as Stoke Road is one of the busiest in Aylesbury. *(K. Vaughan)*

Looking towards town from Hartwell Road, *c.* 1905. This presents a rather rural scene with pigs grazing in the field on the right. The cottages in the distance are those fronting Oxford Road (now Friarage Road). The three children are standing on the bridge that goes over Bear Brook which led to the corn mill (the entrance is at the bottom right). The field has since been built on and the road and bridge have both been widened. *(K. Vaughan)*

Royal Bucks Hospital, *c.* 1905. The foundation stone was laid on 1 May 1861 by Lady Verney. The architect was David Brandon who, as we have seen, also designed many other buildings in Aylesbury. The building was built further back than its predecessor and is much larger. It was constructed behind the old building and was not visible until the old hospital was dismantled and everything sold. There could well be bits of the old infirmary used in the building of houses in the town in the 1860s. *(K. Vaughan)*

The bootmaker's shop of A.E. Felix in Temple Street, *c.* 1905. The building stands on the corner of Temple Street and Temple Square and has a fine example of a late Georgian shopfront. Inside, however, the building is very different as it dates from the Tudor period and has some wonderful carved beams. An estate agent now occupies the former shop. *(K. Vaughan)*

An unusual view of the canal when it was drained for cleaning, *c.* 1905. Viewed from the locks by Park Street this photograph shows how shallow the canal actually is. Further down the canal it had silted up so much that there was no water there at all. The buildings on the left are part of Walton Mill. *(Bucks County Museum)*

A man is taking one of his cattle out of Aylesbury on the Tring Road, *c.* 1905. It is likely he has just come from the market in town. The large factory in the distance is the Printing Works of Hazell, Watson & Viney. On the left is the entrance to the cemetery. Opposite are houses that were built in the late nineteenth century as part of the Victoria Park estate. These were the homes of workers from the Printing Works and the Nestlé factory nearby. *(K. Vaughan)*

The Queens Head in Temple Square, *c.* 1905. Dating from the seventeenth century, this pub is one of the oldest surviving in the town and still retains its original name. (*Bucks County Museum*)

Church Street, *c.* 1905. Over the years, during excavations for various building works, human bones have frequently been discovered, giving rise to the theory that the church burial ground was larger in antiquity than it is today. This street is a lot wider than many of the older thoroughfares in the town and was formerly known as Broad Street. (*R.J. Johnson*)

Some children playing near the prison on Bierton Road, *c.* 1905. With significantly less traffic in those days, children could play in the roads quite safely. How times have changed! *(K. Vaughan)*

Walton Pond, with Walton Road on the left, *c.* 1905. Many of these cottages were occupied by workers of the milk factory and the printing works which were just a short distance away. In September 1940 this whole area was shaken by a landmine (that was dropped by parachute) which fell behind Walton Grange, resulting in the demolition of many of these cottages. *(K. Vaughan)*

The staff of Aylesbury Prison, *c.* 1905. In 1894 the prison was enlarged and in the following year was changed to accommodate only female convicts. In 1903 a Reformatory for inebriates was added. *(R.J. Johnson)*

Aylesbury railway station, *c.* 1905. The station was built in 1863 on the site of some nursery gardens that belonged to Mark De Fraine. It is hard to imagine this area covered in fruit trees. The Aylesbury & Buckingham Railway Company were the first to run the station. Since then, various additions have been made to the line and the original station building was rebuilt and enlarged in 1925. *(R.J. Johnson)*

The Cattle Market, *c.* 1905. The corn stores of Loader & Sons are on the left. They were originally from Thame and came to Aylesbury in 1897. The Cattle Market itself was formed when the Market Company bought the land formerly occupied by the White Hart Hotel in Market Square. The former gardens were an ideal site for the sale of livestock. Today this has all been replaced by a cinema complex. *(K. Vaughan)*

This quiet view of Kingsbury, *c.* 1905, shows the stone and marble works of J.W. Killer, an unfortunate name to be associated with a maker of gravestones. Some examples of his gravestones are seen in front of his building. Over in the corner is the Victoria Club with the Rockwood pub just to the right of it. *(K. Vaughan)*

Looking up Buckingham Road towards town, *c.* 1905. At the top of the hill is the Primitive Methodist Church with Melrose House next to it. These have both since been demolished. Above them the spire of St Mary's Church is just visible. *(R.J. Johnson)*

Bierton Road, *c.* 1905. The villas on the right were built in the 1880s on what used to be orchards. St John's Church is visible at the end of the road. It was demolished in 1970. St Mary's Church can be seen on the horizon. Just beyond the telegraph pole on the left is the Borough Arms pub with the turning for Park Street next to it. *(K. Vaughan)*

Fred Page is standing next to his pony and trap outside the Bear Inn in Walton Street, 1906. This small inn was one of the oldest in town. As well as being the landlord of the Bear, Mr Page was a blacksmith by trade and had his smithy at the rear of the inn. The building survived until the 1960s when, with a lot of other buildings, it was demolished to make way for a roundabout. (*Bucks County Museum*)

Market Square, *c.* 1906. In the foreground is one of the statues of lions that were given to the town in 1887. Originally they stood in the grounds of Waddesdon Manor. Baron Rothschild, the owner, decided to give them to the Infirmary at the top of Buckingham Road. They were going to be sited somewhere in the grounds of the hospital but it was decided that a better place for them would be in the Market Square. In 1888 they were transported by steamroller to the positions where they remain to this day. (*K. Vaughan*)

On 23 June 1906 there was a demonstration in aid of the Lifeboat Saturday Fund. The crew from Deal in Kent paraded the lifeboat named *Tramore* through the town before arriving at the canal basin. It was then ceremoniously launched into the water. People took trips in it as far as the bridge at the High Street. After the boat launch there were various other events including swimming, walking the pole, a tub race, a life-saving race and a polo match. (*K. Vaughan*)

On Friday 27 July 1906 a violent storm visited Aylesbury. The rain descended in torrents and caused flooding to many basements in the High Street area of the town. The view seen here is of Park Street and provided an excellent opportunity for photographers of the day, in this case Mr Steggall of Cambridge Street. (*K. Vaughan*)

Looking down Oxford Road, 1908. These houses fronting the road were built on land formerly occupied by the old Union Workhouse. When the workhouse closed, part of the site was reused as a silk mill. The other part of the site was redeveloped for housing purposes and became Mount Street and Brook Row. The entrance to Mount Street is just where the little girl is standing, opposite the horse and cart. These houses still remain and now front the dual carriageway called Friarage Road. *(Bucks County Museum)*

Temple Square after a heavy fall of snow, Sunday 26 April 1908. The snow started to fall on the evening of Saturday 25th. It must have been quite a shock for people waking up to find everything covered with thick snow. It caused the inevitable havoc and was also a great opportunity to take some picturesque photographs of the town. *(Bucks County Museum)*

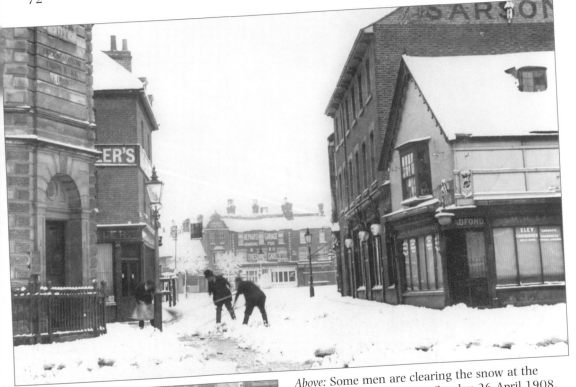

Above: Some men are clearing the snow at the entrance to Kingsbury on Sunday 26 April 1908. The snow did not stay for long as on Monday and Tuesday there was heavy rain to wash it all away. This caused severe flooding in many areas, particularly in the Park Street area where the land is low lying. (*Bucks County Museum*)

On 1 July 1909 there was a procession for the Missionary Festival of the Oxford Diocese. The cross bearer was Mr H. Crump, who was followed by various other clergymen from the Aylesbury area. The procession started from the Town Hall and finished at St Mary's Church where a service was held. (*R.J. Johnson*)

3

Through the War Years
1910–19

New recruits outside the office for the Oxon and Bucks Light Infantry in Temple Square, August 1914.
(Bucks County Museum)

Above: A packed Market Square during the unveiling of the Lord Chesham statue on 14 July 1910. Major-General Lord Chesham was knighted for his service with the Imperial Yeomanry during the Boer War. The statue was sculpted by John Tweed. *(K. Vaughan)*

Some parts of Aylesbury have hardly changed at all over the years and Temple Street is a good example of this. Here we see it in about 1910 looking towards Temple Square. It is also one of the few streets that still has a cobbled surface. *(K. Vaughan)*

These houses in Parsons Fee, pictured in about 1910, are some of the oldest in Aylesbury. The bell turret on the roof shows that this whole row was used as a school-house at the time. *(Bucks County Museum)*

At the rear of the cottages in Parsons Fee was this playground. St Mary's Church can be seen peering over the roof on the left. The cottages have since been converted back into dwellings and the playground is now gardens. *(Bucks County Museum)*

Buckingham Street, 1910. The foundation stone of the Wesleyan Church was laid on 1 June 1893 and opened on 19 April the following year. The church has remained very much the same in appearance except that it no longer has a front wall. On the right are some deckchairs outside the premises of house furnishers Jenns & Son. *(K. Vaughan)*

Bicester Road looking towards town, *c.* 1910. This road has always been a more industrial part of Aylesbury with various workshops and factories being built in the area. The Cubitt car factory had its works immediately to the right of the picture. The sign of the Hop Pole Inn is just visible in the centre and stands on the corner of Southern Road, another industrial area. *(K. Vaughan)*

Looking down Stocklake, *c. 1910*. This picture was taken from the footbridge, built in 1892, which crossed over the railway line. A train is approaching Aylesbury, having come from Cheddington. Little remains of this railway line today but its route is still apparent on the landscape. *(K. Vaughan)*

The yard of Walton Brewery, *c. 1910*. Until 1871 the brewery was run by the Terry family who were highly regarded locally. When Edward Terry retired in that year, the brewery was sold to Messrs Wroughton for about £45,000 – a vast sum at the time. A total of ninety-four inns and public houses were included in the sale. In 1895 the Aylesbury Brewery Company took over the Walton Street site and brewing continued there until about 1935. Today the company no longer exists and the site has been totally redeveloped for offices and housing. *(Bucks County Museum)*

Photographed in about 1910, this end of Buckingham Street appears very different from how it does today. On the left is Fisher's butcher's shop. Next is the Red Cow pub, which had closed by the 1920s. Another pub along this row was the Three Tuns, which is the building on the end with the projecting sign. Then comes the turning into Whitehall Street and on the far right another pub, the Plough. *(Bucks County Museum)*

An Aylesbury Dairy Company delivery man in Putney, London, *c.* 1910. The company was set up by Mr Allender, a gentleman farmer from Buckinghamshire. With the coming of the town's second railway in the 1860s, a good opportunity arose to transport fresh milk from the countryside direct to London. By the end of the nineteenth century various depots were established in the city. *(K. Vaughan)*

The John Hampden statue after completion. It was
unveiled on 27 June 1912 by Lord Rothschild.
The statue was sculpted by Mr H.C. Fehr and a copy
was exhibited at the Royal Academy in the same year.
It was a popular attraction.

John Hampden, a first cousin of Oliver Cromwell,
had refused to pay Ship Money, which was introduced
in 1627 by Charles I. He was imprisoned for a year.
On his release he retired to his country estates. During
the Civil War he fought on the Parliamentarian side in
1643. In that year at Chalgrove he was shot twice in
the shoulder and died six days later of his wounds in
Thame. *(K. Vaughan)*

Below: On 22 September 1913 Winston Churchill, in
his capacity as First Lord of the Admiralty, visited
Aylesbury during army manoeuvres. He is seen here
arriving in Market Square on his way to the George
Hotel where he had dinner and stayed overnight.
The next day he travelled up to Buckingham where
the manoeuvres were held. Various battle scenarios
were carried out which provided vital training for
what was to come. *(Bucks County Museum)*

Soldiers on their way to Buckingham for the army manoeuvres which took place in September 1913. Here they are approaching Buckingham Road having first assembled in the Market Square. The Plough Inn, which was on the corner of Bicester Road and Whitehall Street, is seen on the right. Another pub, the Three Tuns, stood opposite at the end of Buckingham Street. (R. Adams)

Some new recruits march along Wendover Road in 1914, probably on their way to Halton Camp. The pub pictured here is the Three Pigeons, which only disappeared recently to make way for housing. (Bucks County Museum)

Troops take a rest in the courtyard of the Kings Head in 1914. This place is no stranger to the military, as during the Civil War it was where Oliver Cromwell is reputed to have stayed while the garrison was stationed here. *(Bucks County Museum)*

Queen's Park School when it was used as a military hospital during the First World War. Through the railings a man in a wheelchair is seen with five other men – some of many soldiers to be treated there over nearly five years. The last wounded soldier to leave was in August 1919 and the hospital was returned to school usage in the following month. The school has since closed and now the building is an arts centre. Some of the original buildings have been demolished and replaced by housing. *(K. Vaughan)*

The 10th Yorkshire Regiment leaving Aylesbury on Saturday 22 May 1915. Commanded by Colonel A. De S. Hadow, they moved from their billets in Aylesbury, where they were quartered for six months, and proceeded to North Camp at Halton. The battalion paraded at 1.15 p.m., and assembled in force in Cambridge Street, where there were large crowds to see them leave. They were headed by the 2nd Bucks Battalion, the Oxford and Bucks Light Infantry and the Aylesbury Printing Works Band while the band of the 10th Yorkshire occupied a position midway in the ranks. At 1.30 p.m. the command, 'Quick march', was given, and the battalion marched to Market Square, turning down High Street (where we see them pictured here outside the LNER station), and along Tring Road.

When Exchange Street was reached the Territorial band filed into that thoroughfare and played 'Auld Lang Syne' as the troops marched by. The Printing Works Band then escorted the regiment to Halton, and the soldiers quickly arrived at their new quarters. This is a particularly good photograph as it shows some interesting bill posters of the time. Most of them are for Longley's, the drapers and house furnishers in High Street. The large one with 'Whitbread Ales' on it is for J.K. Fowler's wine merchants business in Walton Street. (K. Vaughan)

Soldiers take a break in the High Street on 23 June 1915. The house with the bay windows was then the home of Mrs Ward. The building has since had an extension built over the front garden and is now a record shop. The sign for builders Ward & Cannon can be seen on the left. The Pavilion cinema (now a bingo hall) would later be built on their site. *(Bucks County Museum)*

The top of Cambridge Street and High Street, *c.* 1915. This unusual view is taken from either Lloyds Bank or the George Hotel. The Round House in the foreground was erected when the High Street (then New Road) was built in 1826. On the right is the Crown Hotel. *(Bucks County Museum)*

Kings Road in Queen's Park, *c.* 1915. The school, which takes its name from the estate, is on the right. All the houses opposite look the same and are neatly arranged. Over the years, of course, people have made various alterations to their houses and also, because of the Second World War, all the railings have gone. *(K. Vaughan)*

Highbridge Road looking towards town, *c.* 1915. This view compares well with the one on page 47 which shows the road before any houses were built. At the end of the road is the footbridge over the canal which leads to Highbridge Walk. *(R.J. Johnson)*

Oxford Road, *c.* 1915. This view shows a couple of pubs that have now gone. The Hen & Chickens on the left was rebuilt further back from its original site in 1965. Facing us in the distance is the Rising Sun, which was also demolished in 1965 when this stretch of road was widened and renamed Friarage Road. The entrance to Castle Street is just to the left of the Rising Sun. *(K. Vaughan)*

Some of the houses that were built near the Nestlé factory in the High Street, *c.* 1915. The entrance to Albion Street is visible just before the canal bridge. This is where the Albion Bakery was located until 1976 when it closed. *(R.J. Johnson)*

New Street viewed from the Buckingham Road end, *c.* 1915. Originally this was a track joining Cambridge Street to Buckingham Road. Eventually plots of building ground were sold on the northern side of the road and side roads were added – Fleet Street, Havelock Street and Alexander Road. (*Bucks County Museum*)

Temple Street, *c.* 1915. The group of children on the left are standing outside the picture framer's shop of W. Izzard. On the 1809 map of Aylesbury, Temple Street was known as Cordwainers Row. The street must have been the local centre for boot and shoe-making for some time. (*K. Vaughan*)

A very quiet Buckingham Road, *c.* 1915. The New Zealand Inn is in the centre. On old maps this area was known as New Zealand. Some of the cottages either side of it are pre-Victorian, making this area quite old. At the time of this photograph they overlooked fields towards Bicester Road. In the 1960s Whaddon Chase, Kenilworth Drive, Selkirk Avenue among others were built there. *(Bucks County Museum)*

A group of men from the Medical Corps take a break on their way through Aylesbury in April 1916. This is a postcard sent by one of the men to his wife in Norfolk. He wrote at the end of the message, 'It's the clock tower we sit in front of at Aylesbury Market Square. Will write soon. Goodbye. Russ.' One wonders if he ever did write again. *(K. Vaughan)*

Who said traffic jams were a recent thing? This view from 1916 shows the junction of Buckingham Street with Whitehall Street. It is likely there was some kind of fair on in the town as it was quite unusual to see so many carts converged in one place. (*Bucks County Museum*)

At the end of September 1919 the country had a strike on the railways, causing everything to come to a standstill. Here we see some of the many steam and petrol-driven vehicles waiting to depart from Market Square for their deliveries around the Aylesbury area and for London too. These vehicles were not used very much in those days for the general public. During the First World War they were used a lot in France and at the end of the war many of them were reconditioned for public use. (*Bucks County Museum*)

4

Between the Wars
1920–39

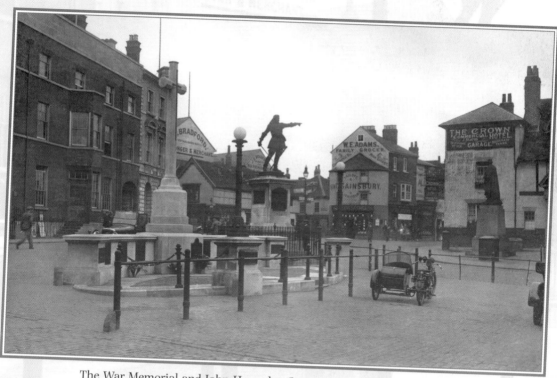

The War Memorial and John Hampden Statue in Market Square, *c.* 1925.
(K. Vaughan)

The teachers and pupils of Temple School, February 1920. The school was then situated in Putnam House, Buckingham Street. Miss Locke started the school in 1880 in Temple Square, hence the name. By the turn of the twentieth century it was taken over by Miss Amery and Miss Gleaves and continued in Temple Square until about 1910 when the school was moved to Putnam House. The house was home

to boarders and it had classrooms at the rear which backed on to New Street. The school also had a kindergarten in Church Street. By 1940 the school had closed and the old building became the Mid-Bucks Shelter & Maternity Home. In 1970 the building was demolished and remained waste ground for a few years until a large office block was erected on the site. *(K. Vaughan)*

High Street looking towards town, *c.* 1920. This view is from the canal bridge, and shows the houses that were built opposite Vale Park. The entrance to Albion Street is on the left in the centre of the photograph. *(K. Vaughan)*

The moulding shop at Walton Engine Works in Walton Road, *c.* 1920. The ironworks were established by William Morris in 1887 and over the years the site produced all sorts of things, including cooking ranges, drain covers and lamp posts. The site was located adjacent to the Millwrights Arms pub and even had its own miniature railway – a very practical idea given the large amount of heavy iron that had to be moved around the place. *(K. Vaughan)*

The Rising Sun in Oxford Road was a quaint old pub dating from the seventeenth century. Here we see it as it was in the 1920s under the ownership of Elizabeth Hall, who is standing in the doorway. Sadly this building was a victim of the 1960s redevelopment and one of the carriageways of Friarage Road now passes through the site. *(R.J. Johnson)*

A view of Kingsbury, *c.* 1920. The First World War German tank in the centre was placed there on 24 March 1920, having been given to the town by the National War Savings Committee. It was a popular attraction for many people although some protested about it being there. In April 1920 Messrs John and Charles Ivatts, who owned a large shoe shop nearby, prepared a petition. It seems this had little effect as the tank remained there until 1929. The drinking fountain in the foreground was put here in 1914 and was designed by Fred Taylor. It too was removed in 1929 and is now situated in Vale Park. *(Bucks County Museum)*

The hairdresser and tobacconist's shop of William Tomkins in Great Western Street, *c.* 1920. The premises were here until 1967 when, during the redevelopment of the area, they were demolished to make way for the present bus station. *(Bucks County Museum)*

The shop of cycle maker Arthur Thomas Adkins in the High Street, *c.* 1920. According to an advertisement of the time he was agent for firms such as BSA, Raleigh, Humber, Globe and Sparkbrook. Later on he sold wireless sets such as the 'Marconiphone' and also televisions. *(C. Watson)*

An advert from the early 1920s. Ivatts were established in the town in 1723 making them one of the oldest businesses in Aylesbury. (*K. Vaughan*)

A moving scene of the unveiling of the War Memorial on 15 September 1921. The Market Square is practically at bursting point with at least 5,000 people watching the proceedings. Even the roofs of the Town Hall and County Hall are occupied by a few men looking over the square. It must have been quite a view from up there. The memorial was unveiled by Lord and Lady Lincolnshire accompanied by Messrs Field, Cannon, and Taylor. Fred Taylor was the architect and the memorial was built of Portland stone by the well-known local building firm Webster & Cannon. In the official programme for the unveiling an 'In Memoriam' note read: 'Today we have a sad and proud duty to perform: sad because the unveiling of a

War Memorial awakens most sorrowful memories in all our hearts, proud because every heart must thrill with pride in recalling the glorious record of the sons of Aylesbury in the Great War, a record which for ever will inspire in the youth of the Borough the noble qualities of steadfastness and fidelity'. There are 264 names of those who lost their lives in the First World War inscribed on the bronze panels at the foot of the cross. On 20 May 1951 a further 106 names were added to commemorate the losses of the Second World War. *(K. Vaughan)*

Grecian Street, *c.* 1920. This road is situated in Victoria Park. These houses were built in 1901 and have a date plate at the end of the row with the name 'Granmer Cottages'. Houses in Queen Street are seen facing. (*K. Vaughan*)

Aylesbury ducks huddled in a back yard, *c.* 1920. Duck breeding is virtually all Aylesbury is known for and breeders were very successful at it. The birds were popular in top London restaurants and were bred in the town and surrounding areas in back yards just like the one shown here. There were also main breeders such as 'Ducky' Weston who bred them in the Oxford Road area of Aylesbury. The duck is still bred in various parts of the UK and is now a rare sight in its home town. (*K. Vaughan*)

Robinsons house furnishers and removals in Silver Street, 1922. In addition to this place, they also had another shop in High Street which would later become their main premises. Silver Lane is off to the right and in Victorian times it had a tallow factory run by Mr Kingham. It was constantly the subject of complaints in the area as it created some noisome fumes. Now this whole area has disappeared as Friars Square has been built on the site. (*Bucks County Museum*)

During the week of 15 to 24 September 1923 the Mayor of Aylesbury, George Thrasher, held a Special Appeal for Funds on behalf of the Royal Bucks Hospital. Various events were held in different parts of the town such as a jumble sale, a concert in the Town Hall, roundabouts in the Market Square and the principal attraction was the trail of pennies which is pictured here in Kingsbury. The trail was laid in other parts of the town too – Cambridge Street, High Street, Buckingham Street, the Recreation Ground, Oxford Road, Church Street, Temple Street, Buckingham Road, Bicester Road and Walton Street. The number of pennies came to 18,286, measured 609 yards and totalled £76 3s 9d. (*Bucks County Museum*)

The Temple Square charabanc ready to depart for the Empire Exhibition, 1924. The exhibition was opened on 23 April by King George V and was held at the British Empire Stadium (later renamed Wembley Stadium). Fifty-six countries took part in the exhibition and it drew large crowds. (*Bucks County Museum*)

Market Square, *c.* 1925. The Bell Hotel is a long-established inn and is seen here shortly after it was enlarged, having had another floor added and the frontage altered. The garages were opposite in Walton Street behind Samuels corner shop. The shop was demolished along with everything else in Great Western Street in 1967 to make way for Friars Square shopping centre. *(K. Vaughan)*

An aerial view of the centre of Aylesbury, *c.* 1925. It shows a busy day in Market Square and gives a good view of the old town. The Bell Hotel is at the bottom centre with Silver Street stretching up towards Temple Street off to the left. Kingsbury is visible at the top left of the picture. *(R.J. Johnson)*

The fine old hall in the Kings Head, *c.* 1925. This fifteenth-century inn was sold in 1872 to Baron Rothschild when the owner, Jesse Ward, died. It stayed in the Rothschild family until 1926 when the National Trust took over. *(K. Vaughan)*

The Bulls Head Hotel, *c.* 1925. Situated in the Market Square, this old inn was established in 1478. The façade was added in the 1920s by the owner, Mr Gargini. He took over the running of the place in 1913 after having run the White Hart Hotel in Buckingham. The passage to the right led to the stables and gardens. Also to the rear was Hale Leys Passage which linked the High Street to the Market Square. The name of Hale Leys is preserved in the shopping centre which now stands on the site of the Bulls Head. Some more views of this old building are on pages 125 and 126. *(K. Vaughan)*

Above: On the corner of Friarage Road and Great Western Street stood this handsome Victorian pub, the Falcon, which is pictured here in about 1925. It was built at the time when Great Western Street was formed in the 1860s by the opening of the new railway. When this whole area was flattened for the construction of Friars Square in the 1960s, the licence was transferred to the Steeplechase in Southcourt. *(Bucks County Museum)*

The statue of Benjamin Disraeli in Market Square, *c.* 1925. It was unveiled on 6 September 1923 by Lord Cottesloe and was provided by public subscription. Disraeli was Member of Parliament for Buckinghamshire from 1847 to 1876. He also gave money towards the building of the Clock Tower. *(R. Adams)*

Above: These small cottages stood in Upper Hundreds, an area of the town which was very ancient. The buildings at the far end are in Anchor Lane, just on the corner of Britannia Street. The double doors on the far right were the entrance to the Salvation Army hut. *(Bucks County Museum)*

Looking down Whitehall Row towards Whitehall Street. Some of these cottages were very old and must have been tiny inside. These, along with the cottages in Upper Hundreds, were deemed unfit for habitation in July 1925 and were all demolished. Many of the families from these cottages were moved into new houses that were built on Oxford Road. *(Bucks County Museum)*

Some more cottages in the vicinity of Upper Hundreds. These were in Nags Head Passage which took its name from the pub that stood nearby on Cambridge Street. These cottages were occupied by mainly poor families and in the 1920s the town council decided that these dwellings were unhealthy places and these too met their end. *(Bucks County Museum)*

Below: Looking down the High Street from Market Square, *c.* 1925. The Crown Hotel was one of Aylesbury's oldest and best-known hostelries and originally stretched right across before the High Street (then New Road) was built in 1826. Part of the old building is seen on the right and gives some idea of how it used to look. Its layout would have been similar to the Kings Head, having a central gateway leading to stables and gardens at the rear. In the late 1930s this fine old place was demolished and replaced by shops. *(K. Vaughan)*

On 15 May 1926 HRH Princess Mary visited Aylesbury to open the new Girl Guides Hall in Beaconsfield Road. The Princess arrived at the Town Hall where the area was filled with cheering crowds. After various addresses in the Town Hall the procession through the town took them down the High Street to Queen's Park and up to the entrance to the new hall. A great ceremony was held at the hall, and afterwards in Walton Road (pictured here) there was a grand march-past of all the many companies of Girl Guides. Her Royal Highness took the salute together with Mrs F.T. Higgins Bernard, the County Commissioner, as the girls filed by to the music of the Territorial Band. *(K. Vaughan)*

Walton Street, 1928. The large building in the centre was the residence of the Chief Constable. Shortly after this photo was taken, this building along with those further down the road would be demolished to make way for new County Offices. *(Bucks County Museum)*

Walton Street in 1928. This fine row of Victorian houses was built in about 1850 when the Old Gaol was demolished and the site sold. They stood here until 1929 when the County Offices were built on the site. *(Bucks County Museum)*

Cambridge Street in the late 1920s, viewed from the Park Street entrance. The building on the corner was the local post office and bakery run by Stevens & Son. A little further up the street is Jack Tofield's garage. He later moved round the corner into Park Street. *(K. Vaughan)*

The Duke of York (later George VI) visiting Southcourt on 2 July 1928 to open one of the first four houses built in York Place. On that day he also visited the Printing Works of Hazell, Watson & Viney and the Trades and Industrial Exhibition for Civic Week. *(K. Vaughan)*

Bicester Road during Aylesbury Civic Week, 1928. The factory buildings seen here were formerly used by the car makers Cubitt. *(Bucks County Museum)*

Aylesbury Fire Brigade in 1928. The station was situated in Bourbon Street, just up from the Public Baths. In about 1943 they moved to a new site on Cambridge Street. Just recently they have moved again to a newly built station in Stocklake. *(Bucks County Museum)*

An aerial view of Aylesbury, *c.* 1930. Castle Street is seen meeting up with Temple Square in the centre. Above to the left is Kingsbury with the bus station which was a recent addition. St Mary's Church is just visible on the far left. The High Street which curves down to meet Market Square is at the top on the right. *(Bucks County Museum)*

The corner of Exchange Street and Walton Street, 1930. These buildings were part of Aylesbury police station and were rebuilt in 1935. The building on the end of the row on the left still exists today and is undergoing renovation work. Beyond are County Offices which opened in 1929. *(Bucks County Museum)*

Exchange Street, 1930. This street was formed in October 1864 and crossed land that once formed part of the grounds of the Old Gaol and the White Hart Hotel. The buildings seen here are part of Aylesbury police station; the one on the far left is the one shown above. These were demolished in 1935 when a new one was built on the same site. To the far right of the photograph is the entrance to the cattle market. *(Bucks County Museum)*

The County Hall in Market Square was designed by the noted architect Sir John Vanbrugh, and was built in about 1737. The window at the far left end of the hall was originally a doorway which led to the Old Gaol and House of Correction. This doorway was filled in when the gaol premises were demolished in the late 1840s. This view from the 1930s shows well how popular the motor car had become with the square being used for parking. Soon Aylesbury would be altered almost beyond recognition because of the need for wider roads and roundabouts. *(K. Vaughan)*

Market Square in the 1930s. The ivy-covered building is Bedford House and is home to Barclays Bank. They moved into the building in 1919 and are there to this day. Note the pigs being led from under the arches. With the cattle market being just behind the Town Hall, it was not an uncommon sight in those days to see livestock being taken there from the Market Square. *(K. Vaughan)*

Above: A busy Kingsbury in the early 1930s. The bus station was established there in 1929 and at first consisted of a small island with a telephone box in the centre. Later on, in 1938, a large bus shelter was added and the island was enlarged. In the late 1960s the bus station moved to its present site in Great Western Street. *(K. Vaughan)*

The Kings Head, 1933. This is the fine old gateway through to the courtyard at the rear. The gateway is one of the oldest surviving portions of the building, which has had many additions to it over the centuries. The old hall is just to the left of the entrance and boasts a fine stained-glass window dating from the fifteenth century. *(K. Vaughan)*

Above: The staff and family of bakers Page & Son outside their Buckingham Street shop, 25 September 1934. Page's were top class bakers in Aylesbury and frequently won trophies for their bakery skills. The shop opened in 1904 when Mr Edward E. Page took over the business from Mr Kingham. The business closed in the early 1980s and the building was demolished to make way for offices and shops. *(K. Vaughan)*

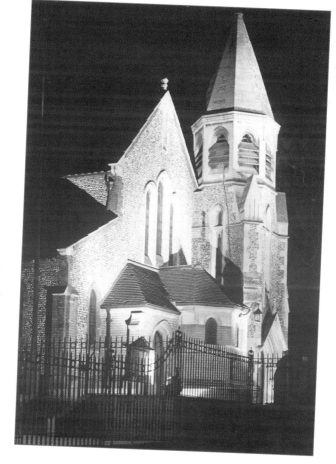

Holy Trinity Church in Walton Street lit up for the Women's Electrical Association Ball on 19 February 1935. In the evening there was a whist drive and dance next door in Walton Parish Hall. Music for dancing was supplied by the Black Aces and they apparently did a fine job with both the modern music and with the more traditional tunes. The association was set up in 1925 to help women in the home become familiar with using electricity as it was becoming a more standard form of energy. *(Bucks County Museum)*

The next few photographs show parts of the town decorated for the Jubilee of King George V on 6 May 1935. Here we see a Shell Oil lorry, which was driven by Joseph 'Boney' Clark, in Cambridge Street. It is not known whether Clark is in the picture. *(Bucks County Museum)*

Looking down Buckingham Street during the coronation festivities in 1936. This array of flags is outside Chamberlin's Motor Engineers, seen on the left. *(C. Watson)*

An address by Canon Howard was read in St Mary's Church and followed by a service. There was a procession from the church afterwards, which is seen here in Church Street. *(Centre for Bucks Studies)*

Market Street was so narrow that it was an ideal place for this kind of display. The decorations extended into Bourbon Street and beyond. *(C. Watson)*

Here we see the decorations of Longleys the drapers in High Street. This view shows just a small portion of their display as their premises were very extensive and the whole shopfront would have been covered. (C. Watson)

Market Square was lavishly decorated during the coronation festivities in 1936. Here we see gentlemen's outfitters Foster Brothers giving a fine display. (C. Watson)

The Red Lion in Kingsbury, *c. 1935*. This building is one of the oldest in Aylesbury. There is evidence of there being an inn on the site in the sixteenth century as in mid-Victorian times, when work was being done to the basement, part of a beer measure was found inscribed with the words 'Ann Rogers, ye Red Lyon, 1569'. The building still remains today although it has lost its original name and the central gateway has been built over. Next to the Red Lion on the left were corn merchants Seth Wheeler & Sons, who later were taken over by another corn merchant, Loader's. *(R.J. Johnson)*

Cambridge Street, *c. 1935*. This scene shows one of Aylesbury's old inns before it was refronted a few years later. The Windmill had been there for many years. Many pubs in the town were owned by the Aylesbury Brewery Company but this one was under another local brewery, Hopcraft & Norris. Today the building is occupied by a veterinary surgery. *(Bucks County Museum)*

Above: The next four photographs give a tour round the Bulls Head Hotel in Market Square as it appeared in 1936. Here we see the restaurant. The proprietor at the time was Mr Gargini. The building was very old and some parts dated from the fifteenth century. As is common with many old established hotels, it was added to and extended. Apparently there were old ship's timbers built into the structure. *(K. Vaughan)*

The smoking lounge was another room with finely carved beams. During the time Mr Gargini was there he modernised the hotel and gave it a mock-Tudor façade. A view of the front can be seen on page 108. *(K. Vaughan)*

To the rear of the hotel were the garages and beyond there was this pleasant garden. The large building facing us is the rear of the Congregational Church in the High Street. When the hotel was demolished in the late 1960s this garden became a car park along with the rest of the old site. Hale Leys Shopping Centre stands here today. (*K. Vaughan*)

Another addition to the hotel was this large assembly hall. It was a popular place for wedding receptions and dances over the years. What a shame it is all now gone – it would have been an asset to the town. (*K. Vaughan*)

Looking towards Market Square from the High Street, *c. 1937*. Montague Burton's menswear shop opened in 1936. The building must have looked amazing in the sunshine with its white Art Deco façade. Traffic lights were installed in the mid-1930s at the end of the High Street and were a contributing factor to the demise of the Crown Hotel which is immediately on the left. Apparently guests staying there were frequently put off by the traffic noise and fumes. It is a sad irony that the hotel had undergone extensive refurbishment about this time and yet it was all pulled down by the end of 1939. *(R.J. Johnson)*

The Vale swimming pool in the late 1930s. This area was used by the Vale of Aylesbury Cycling and Athletic Club until 1929 when the ground was purchased by the Corporation. The swimming pool was opened by the Mayor, Councillor G. Gargini, on 27 June 1935. Vale Park did not open until 1 July 1937. *(K. Vaughan)*

ACKNOWLEDGEMENTS

What a fascinating project this has been. It has taken over a year to compile and has involved many long evenings! I am so pleased to have had use of photographs from the Bucks County Museum and the Centre for Local Studies. It has been quite a task selecting the best ones for this book. I have also used many photographs from my own collection, which is still growing.

Mr R.J. Johnson has provided me with some useful photographs for which I am very thankful. Miss M. Sale gets my thanks also for the use of some of her photographs, as does Mr R. Adams for promoting my work in his shop – people are always asking him when the next book is coming out so I hope this book fits the bill. I would like to also thank Mrs C. Watson for lending me some of her photographs. If you've enjoyed the book and have any photographs that you want to get rid of or think I might be interested in, please contact the publisher who will forward your details to me. Or alternatively, if you know me, just speak to me!

Hazells Printing Works Band at the factory entrance. This view was taken from a postcard inviting people to listen to the band on the National Programme on 11 June 1938. Note the fine display of trophies in the front row. (*K. Vaughan*)